THE

FLORAL

STENCIL BOOK

*A UNIQUE COLLECTION OF READY-TO-USE STENCILS
IN CLASSIC DESIGNS BY*

JANE THOMSON

LOUISE DRAYTON

HOW TO BEGIN PP. 2–7

ROPE & ROSE SWAG PP. 20–23

MEDIEVAL IRIS PP. 8–11

*LAUREL TREE & GINGER JAR
PP. 16–19*

VICTORIAN LEAVES & LILIES PP. 24–27

ROCOCO LATTICE PP. 12–15

DK

DORLING KINDERSLEY

London • New York • Sydney • Moscow

MIX & MATCH PP. 28–31

How to Begin

STENCILLING IS AN ANCIENT decorative technique and is easy to master. Once you understand how to do it, you will find that stencilling a pattern takes very little time. First, choose your design. Then measure the surface you want to stencil and decide how and where to use the pattern. Experiment with different colours and backgrounds to give your design another look, and try masking and combining other motifs with your stencil to build a unique design. You can use your stencils just about anywhere, and – with a little imagination – create hundreds of designs.

STARTING TO STENCIL

BEFORE YOU BEGIN any project, start with a simple design and practise on lining paper. Begin with the dry stages: gather the equipment you will need, and then cut your sponges and stencils. Mask the edges of the stencil. Next, the wet stages: experiment with paint consistency and sponging, then practise dabbing on scrap paper.

LINING PAPER

LARGE RULER

PLUMB LINE

HOME-MADE PLUMB LINE

Make your own plumb line with a small weight and string

SET SQUARE

EMULSION

METALLIC PAINT

TUBE ACRYLIC

FABRIC MEDIUM

SOLVENT

SCISSORS

TRACING PAPER

SCRAP PAPER

MASKING TAPE

SCALPEL

SPIRIT LEVELS

DENSE FOAM SPONGES

Bottled acrylic paints are easy to use and dry very quickly

Use special paints for ceramics and glass

ACRYLICS

CERAMIC PAINTS

ERASER

PERMANENT PENS

SOFT PENCILS

PAINT BRUSHES

TAPE MEASURE

PAINT DISHES

STENCILLING EQUIPMENT

The most basic equipment for any type of stencilling is a pair of scissors, sponge, tape, ruler, pen, soft pencils, paper, paint and dish, and paint brush. For more complex designs you may need additional materials.

Make sure the dome is smooth and even

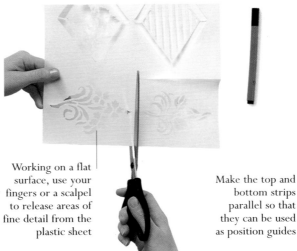

Working on a flat surface, use your fingers or a scalpel to release areas of fine detail from the plastic sheet

Make the top and bottom strips parallel so that they can be used as position guides

1 Cut the sponge into 35-mm and 65-mm (1½-in and 2½-in) squares; trim off the tops to create a smooth dome shape. Make some of the domes smaller for fine detail.

2 Trace the guidelines from the page behind each plastic stencil sheet; cut out and number each stencil. Remove remaining cutouts in the design with a scalpel.

3 Tape strips of tracing paper 5 cm (2 in) wide to each side to prevent paint from smudging all over your surface. Cover parts of the stencil you will not need (see p.6).

Watery paint will drip off your sponge and can ruin your stencil design

The paint should be the consistency of cream

Too much thick paint makes a dense, heavy colour with no pattern marks from the sponge

Watery paint creates a washed-out colour with small bubbles

This paint is the right consistency to produce a textured pattern

4 *It is very important that your paint is mixed to a creamy consistency. Bottled acrylics should be about right, but you may have to thin other types of paint.*

5 *Test the consistency of your paints by dabbing the sponge lightly onto scrap paper. Paint of the right consistency will produce an evenly stippled texture.*

WATERY PAINT

The paint shown here is too watery and, because it has seeped under the stencil, all the details are lost — a disastrous result.

Dipping the sponge into the paint dish is the easiest way to apply paint

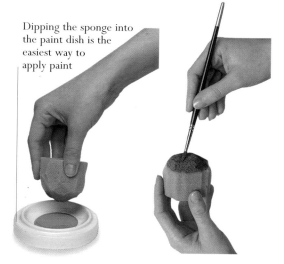

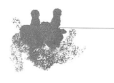

This paint has not been worked evenly into the sponge, producing a blotchy texture

Coverage is better, but extra dabbing on the same spot would work the paint in

This paint has been applied well and the texture is uniform

6 *Apply a little paint to the rounded dome of a dry sponge. You can either dab the sponge lightly into a dish of paint, or use a brush to coat the sponge.*

7 *Before doing your stencil, dab the sponge up and down in the same place on scrap paper to work in all the excess paint. Dab in one area, then below to test.*

8 *The sponge must be smooth and evenly coated with paint to produce an even texture with no blotches.*

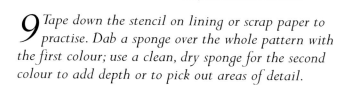

10 *When you have applied all your chosen colours, hold the stencil in place with one hand, and carefully peel it back with the other to inspect the design more clearly. Replace the stencil if you need to make any colour corrections.*

Each time you add more paint to your sponge, remember to re-test the distribution of the paint; aim for an even texture

9 *Tape down the stencil on lining or scrap paper to practise. Dab a sponge over the whole pattern with the first colour; use a clean, dry sponge for the second colour to add depth or to pick out areas of detail.*

A successful stencil has crisp, well-defined edges and graduated colours

USING YOUR STENCILS

Choosing a pattern is the first step in using your stencils. Decide where you want to use your design, and select your colour scheme. Do you want a bold all-over pattern, a bright picture rail, or a striking motif to act as a focal point in a room? Depending on your choices, you may need to master a variety of techniques, such as measuring, repeating, and mitring. After you have completed a project, clean your stencils, repair any damage, and store the stencils flat for the next use. With care, your stencils can be used again and again.

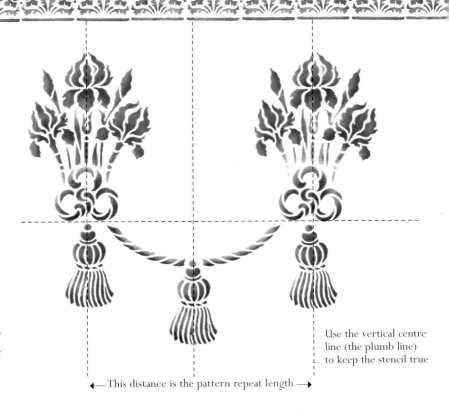

MEASURING THE PATTERN

Before you apply a pattern to any surface, stencil a sample on lining paper as a guide. Mark the centre line and the base-line of the main part of the design on the lining paper, then mark and measure the distance to the pattern's repeat.

← This distance is the pattern repeat length →

Use the vertical centre line (the plumb line) to keep the stencil true

SPACING THE PATTERN

Measure your surface and work out the number of repeats. To avoid stencilling on a corner, add extra space between repeats.

CLOSING UP THE PATTERN

You may need to alter the pattern to make it fit your surface; to include more repeats, close up the space between design elements.

STRETCHING THE PATTERN

Leave wider gaps between parts of the stencil to stretch it; these should be consistent, and will not be noticeable from a distance.

A box-like motif is particularly easy to mitre around a door or window

A large design flanked by another pattern repeated on each side creates a dramatic, harmonious look

Use an existing picture rail as a guide for positioning your design — or stencil a picture rail

Stencil a continuous border just below the ceiling if you want to make it seem lower

Create a dado and enliven a room with a stencil placed about 90 cm (3 ft) above the floorboards

Repeat a bold design around a door or in a hallway; vary the height to suit the space

Make the most of skirting-boards by stencilling a bright pattern just above them

STENCILLING A ROOM

Planning ahead is essential if you are considering an overall stencilling scheme. Sketch your room, draw in your ideas, and hang practice stencils to judge their effect and colour. If you intend to stencil for several hours, add a slow-dry medium to your paints so that they won't dry out.

TESTING COLOURWAYS

Check that the colours you have chosen produce the desired effect by stencilling onto a sample of your wall colour or wallpaper. Depending on the background, colours can appear completely different.

ALIGNMENT

If you need a vertical rule to align a pattern, hang a plumb line above the stencil area, place a ruler against the string, and draw in the line with soft pencil or chalk; erase the lines later.

EQUAL SPACING

Do one stencil and position the second so that the tracing-paper mask around the plastic stencil overlaps the first stencil: trace a few lines. Do the next stencil, then move it on. Match the tracings with the second stencil.

MITRING

Place the set square at the point where horizontal and vertical base-lines intersect

Slightly overlap the previous stencil to ensure there is no gap between the mitred elements of the design

Successful mitring depends on the two base-lines being accurately drawn at a 90° angle

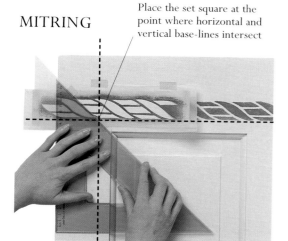

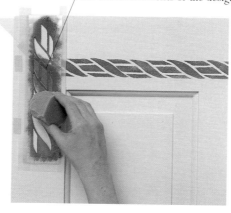

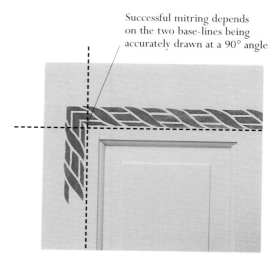

1 *Working from pencilled base-lines, use a set square to position a tracing-paper mask at 45° across the end of the stencil. Tape it to the stencil, and dab in paint.*

2 *Finish the horizontal pattern, then blot the stencil, keeping the mask in place. Flip the stencil, position it on the vertical base-line, and dab in paint.*

3 *Carefully peel back the stencil when the paint is dry. After removing the stencil, rub out the horizontal and vertical base-lines with a very soft eraser.*

CARING FOR YOUR STENCILS

Stencils are delicate and need to be handled with care. Remove tape and masks gently, and wash the stencils after each use. The inked numbers may rub off, so renew them as needed. Store the stencils flat between sheets of paper.

1 *Clean off dried acrylic paints with methylated spirits. Use a paint brush to ease off the paint.*

2 *Soak the stencils in warm soapy water, and rinse in clean water. Dry them flat between light cotton towels.*

REPAIRING DAMAGED STENCILS

Some of the stencil designs are very intricate, and they may develop small rips or tears if the stencils are not handled properly. This type of damage is easy to repair.

1 *Start by covering the tear on both sides of the stencil with masking tape. Be sure the stencil is perfectly flat.*

2 *Using a scalpel or craft knife, carefully cut along the edge of the design. Peel away any excess tape.*

PAINT EFFECTS

How you use your paints will completely transform the look of your stencils. Simply mixing colours is easy – use a brush to mix them, and keep a record of the quantities you use. Try blending, highlighting, and shading, and enjoy experimenting to achieve the style that suits you best.

Complete the blending of colours for the whole design before peeling back the stencil

BLENDING COLOURS

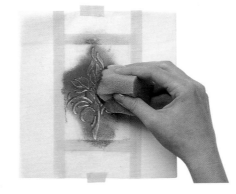

1 Start by sponging the base colour, which should be the lightest shade, over the first stencil. Apply the paint evenly over the entire pattern, then apply a little extra colour to areas of fine detail.

2 Use a clean sponge for the next colour to avoid muddying the paints. To create a richer and more interesting texture, stipple the second darker colour in areas that will be in shadow, such as the undersides of buds.

3 Gently remove the stencil, checking that colours are pleasing. If the stencil is to be repeated, match the colour density and tone of the first stencil, but bear in mind that slight variations are quite attractive.

CREATING VOLUME

1 Shadows will always be opposite your light source. Sponge the lightest colour over the stencil, leaving some areas scarcely painted where the light would fall. Define the edges of the jar with denser colour.

2 Use a clean sponge for the midtone. Stipple this second colour lightly over the first, but avoid the light area. Let some of the first colour show through, but gradually deepen the colour towards the edge to be in shadow.

3 With a clean sponge, stencil the darkest colour in areas of fine detail and deep shadow, such as the neck of the jar. Strive for a gradual but strong contrast between light and dark colours.

MASKING A STENCIL

The simplest way to create a mask is to tape a piece of tracing paper over the part of the design you will not be using. Masking allows you to isolate part of a design or colour areas that need to be distinct, to simplify a complicated pattern, or to substitute one part of a stencil for another.

A simple motif isolated from a larger pattern can be sophisticated and elegant

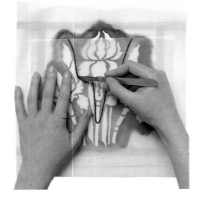

1 Begin by covering the design with tracing paper, and outline the areas you will not be using. With a pair of scissors or a scalpel, cut out part of the tracing paper to uncover the motif to be stencilled.

2 Fasten the mask to the stencil with tape so that the area you want to colour in is exposed. Position the stencil on your surface, and dab in paint.

3 The empty area that had been covered by the mask can be stencilled with a variety of motifs; here, you could use foliage or other flowers.

STENCILLING ON OTHER MATERIALS

Almost any surface can be stencilled – from bare plaster walls to fabric, wood, ceramics, and glass. All of these can be sponged with acrylic or specialist paints (follow the instructions carefully; some ceramic paints may need to baked). Areas that need to be protected can be varnished.

FABRICS

Stencil onto silk, muslin, cotton, or canvas

PAINT CONSISTENCY
Do not thin the paint you use on fabrics, as it is easier to use when thick. To prevent bleeding, add a commercial fabric medium.

USING BLOTTERS
When stencilling lightweight fabrics, such as muslin or silk, use a blotter of absorbent paper or remnants beneath the fabric in case the paint soaks through.

WOODS

Bare wood   Primer and undercoat   Emulsion/acrylic base coat

You can stencil directly onto bare wood or board, but a wood-stained surface will create a rich background

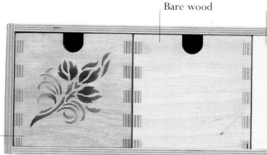

Apply the stencil after the base coat; seal with clear matte varnish if extra protection is needed

BARE WOOD
Prepare the wood surface with sandpaper or wire wool, and wipe clean. Stencil the design. If you want a richly coloured, polished effect, treat the wood with beeswax after stencilling.

PAINTED WOOD
Sand the wood before you begin. Prime it, sand the surface, paint an undercoat, then sand again. Brush after each sanding. Paint the background colour; when dry, stencil your design.

CERAMICS, METAL, AND GLASS

UNGLAZED CERAMICS
Unglazed ceramics, such as terracotta pots or tiles, can be stencilled with acrylic or ceramic paints. Follow the manufacturer's instructions. For a weathered look, rub gently with wire wool.

GLASS AND GLAZED CERAMICS
Stencil directly onto glass with ceramic paints, but make sure the glass is completely clean. Tape residues or fingerprints will prevent the paint from adhering.

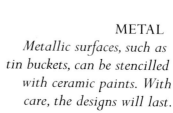

METAL
Metallic surfaces, such as tin buckets, can be stencilled with ceramic paints. With care, the designs will last.

Medieval Iris

Iris was the Greek goddess of the rainbow and the messenger of the gods. This iris stencil was inspired by a medieval manuscript, itself probably derived from the fact that the iris was adopted by the French king Louis VII during the Crusades; the motif evolved from the *fleur-de-Louis* (flower of Louis) to the stylized, tripartite *fleur-de-lis* whose three petals symbolized the virtues of faith, wisdom, and valour. Shakespeare referred to it as *fleur-de-luce* (flower of light), recalling the connection to the Greek goddess. From about 1890, the iris was a favourite of the Arts and Crafts movement, whose goal was to reassert the value of handmade objects over those that were mass-produced. Artists created sinuous, curvilinear designs and flowing forms inspired by nature, a look you can easily replicate by combining the vase with an art nouveau frame border (Stencil 23).

Choose your design to fit the shape harmoniously; use colours to enhance the effect.

Stencil the three flowers and buds, starting with the lightest colour; stencil the foliage next

Cut the stencil here if you find it easier

1 *Mask off the vase from Stencil 1, leaving the irises. Drop a plumb line, and draw a vertical line on which to position the centre of the design. Decide on the height of the design, and stencil the flowers.*

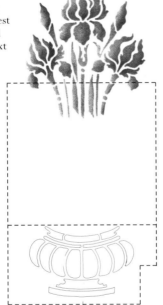

2 *Draw a horizontal base-line below the irises where the vase will sit. Unmask the vase from Stencil 1 and mask off the irises. Mark a centre point just below the vase, and align with the vertical plumb line. Stencil the vase on the base-line.*

Centre point on the stencil aligns with the plumb line

The petals in the centre of the flower are in shade, so use a deeper colour here; use the same colour to define the lower tips of the petals

3 *Mask off the curled end of Stencil 3, then mask off a length of stem so that it will fit between the irises and the vase. Stencil both stems the same distance from the plumb line, then add Stencil 4 between them.*

Shade one side of the vase and the underside of the base for a more realistic effect

If the colours of petals and leaves overlap, it enhances the effect – leaves may have lilac shadows

If you want to fill gaps, use Stencil 2

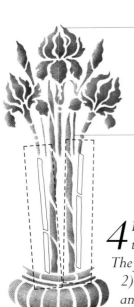

4 *Repeat Stencil 4 from the irises to the vase. The finest stems (Stencil 2) can be used to fill in any remaining gaps.*

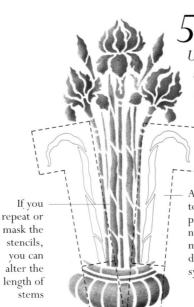

5 *Finish by adding the iris leaves (Stencil 3). Unmask the curved ends, and stencil a leaf on either side of the stems.*

If you repeat or mask the stencils, you can alter the length of stems

Angle slightly to create a pleasing natural effect; make sure the design is symmetrical

6 *Use the darker colours from the flowers in the shadows of the vase; this will unify the overall design.*

1

2

3

Trace the guidelines from this page onto the plastic stencil sheet. Cut along the vertical line of perforations that attaches the sheet to the book. Cut out and number each stencil. Place each one on card before removing any remaining infills with a scalpel.

4

Medieval Iris Variations

SUNLIT IRISES IN VASE: STENCILS 1, 2, 3, 11

ROSE & IRIS BOUQUET: STENCILS 1, 14A

This design, and the one on the right, would make an effective *trompe l'oeil* just above a shelf or mantelpiece, especially if you use realistic colours: soft, muted greens and autumnal shades

You can extend the bouquet to fit a niche or alcove; follow the form of the existing architecture for the best effects

ROSE & TASSEL SPRAY: STENCILS 1, 11, 13, 30

The pyramid shape of this iris design gives it strength and formality, and would be effective stencilled in a single colour (white or gold) on a dark background

IRIS SWAG BORDER: STENCILS 1, 13, 15, 30

GOLDEN TRIUMPHAL BORDER: STENCILS 1, 11

PURPLE IRISES IN VASE: STENCILS 1, 3

TALL IRIS BOUQUET: STENCILS 1, 2, 3, 4, 13, 30

The stencil looks best if you decide on an overall colour scheme and create light and shade from the same hue, rather than using too many different colours

To avoid unsightly gaps, the lower spaces are filled with thicker stems and leaves (Stencils 3 and 4)

Try to use colours to balance the design; here, the three points of the triangular bouquet are dark, and create a strong structure

IRIS & CROCUS BORDER: STENCILS 1, 3, 5, 8

Combining flowers of similar hues looks more pleasing than a garish variety

Rococo Lattice

THE WORD "ROCOCO" describes a style characterized by delicate, profuse ornamentation, and flowers lend themselves very easily to this particular treatment. The crocus was used as a perfume, medicine, dye, and condiment, and the stamens of one species were used to manufacture a dye of brilliant yellow, saffron, symbolizing nobility. Carnations were used in Renaissance betrothal portraits, and in China the flower was a symbol of marriage. The celandine is a well-known harbinger of spring. Whatever the season, this design – especially if you use pastel colours – will create a sense of spring-like cheer in any room.

The floral lattice enlivens a cupboard, and harmonizes with the stencilled storage jars.

1 Using Stencil 7, cut a mask from tracing paper to cover the celandine in the diamond (see p. 6). Mark a horizontal line on the wall, then stencil the diamonds in a row; make sure they are equidistant.

2 You should now have a row of diamonds: one striped, one blank. Next, place the striped diamond stencil over each empty diamond frame. Dab in the stripes to fill the entire row.

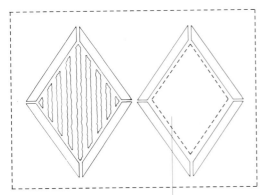

The mask covers only the flower but leaves the frame

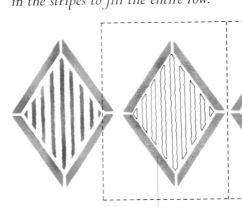

Use a light colour over the frames, and then define the corners with a darker hue; make sure the diamonds are straight and equidistant (see p. 5)

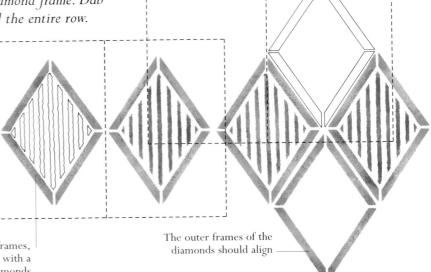

The outer frames of the diamonds should align

3 Now stencil a blank diamond above and below the striped diamonds. The outer frames of the overall pattern (that is, four diamonds) should align.

4 Stencil the crocuses, Stencil 5, in the upper blank diamond. Don't worry if paint for the leaves and petals overlaps: highlights enhance the leaves, and the mixed colours add depth and interest to the design.

5 Fill in the bottom diamonds with carnations (Stencil 6). Emphasize the tips of the leaves and the centre of the flowers with darker hues using a finely tipped sponge for this detailed work.

6 Stencil the border (Stencil 8) on a continuous horizontal line drawn at a suitable distance below the bottom diamonds. Stencil the stripes first.

Position the flowers inside the blank upper and lower diamonds

Make sure that the lower diamonds all align with each other along a horizontal line

5

6

7

Trace the guidelines from this page onto the plastic stencil sheet. Cut along the vertical line of perforations that attaches the sheet to the book. Cut out and number each stencil. Place each one on card before removing any remaining infills with a scalpel.

8

Rococco Lattice Variations

DIAMOND FLORAL BORDER: STENCILS 6, 8

Dab in colours from the flowers and foliage in the border to create a coherent, balanced design

GARDEN PATH BORDER: STENCILS 8, 25, 26

Stencil all the leaves first, then complete the design with the flowers

Keep the colour of the diamond centres quite soft by dabbing colour lightly around the edges — the central motif will show up better

Deepen the colours at the base and top edges

CELANDINE LATTICE: STENCIL 7

Emphasize the four corners of each diamond with a darker colour

Choose the flower whose natural colour complements your room

These strong stripes help create a dramatic border

DIAMOND FLORAL BORDER: STENCILS 5, 6, 7

CARNATION SPRAY: STENCIL 6

Mask off the diamond frame and half the lattice, leaving the longest stripe to create this stencil

Stencil the upper and lower flowers first, then fill in the left and right ones – this design can look quite striking around a door handle

Darken the flowers and the bases of the stems

The bases of the triangles should be slightly darker to create a strong foundation

PLOUGHED FIELD & TREE BORDER: STENCILS 8, 25

DIAMOND & LATTICE BORDER: STENCILS 7, 8

Laurel Tree & Ginger Jar

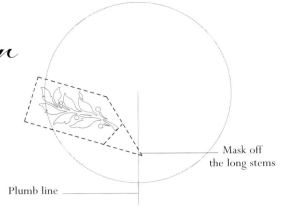

Mask off
the long stems

Plumb line

BECAUSE IT IS AN EVERGREEN, the laurel has been a symbol of immortality for thousands of years. It was sacred to Apollo, the Greek god of music, poetry, prophecy, and medicine, and was worn by Roman emperors during their triumphal entries into the city. The laurel wreath symbolizes an honoured poet (hence the phrase "poet laureate") as well as excellence in the arts and sciences. Ginger, too, has an exalted history: in the seventeenth and eighteenth century, its root was considered a great delicacy, and its desirability and status were reflected in the magnificent, ornately decorated jars that were used by the Chinese to ship this precious condiment to Europe. This versatile design can be used as a decorative element in many contexts.

1 Draw a circle 32 to 45 cm (13 to 18 in) in diameter; then, using a plumb line, draw a line down from the centre point. Fan the leaves (Stencil 11) from left to right around the edge of the circle.

Place the leaves in about the same position on the edge of the circle

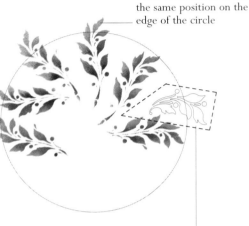

2 Using Stencil 10, fill any remaining gaps. The leaves should cross the pencilled line occasionally, and you should leave enough space in the centre to fill it with leaves. Also, leave a space at the base of the circle for the stem.

Fill in as many gaps as possible, and stencil the centre last; flip some of the leaves to create a more natural, random effect

3 Lift out the poppies on the lower part of the jar (Stencil 9). Centre the jar and dab in the lightest colour. Try to leave the central area fairly light, and use a darker shade near the base and on one side to create a realistic, three-dimensional effect.

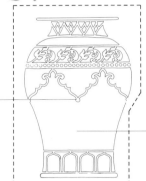

Leaving this area light and darkening the right-hand edge will make the jar seem rounder

Stick this part down with a small amount of blue tack or rolled masking tape to prevent curling

Try varying the shades of green on the laurel leaves to create a more naturalistic effect

4 Using Stencil 12, mask off the required length of stem to fill the gap between the jar and the leaf ball. The stem should start just above the rim of the jar.

Use the terracotta colour of the jar in the leaves for an autumnal effect

For a crisp, well-defined design, pick out areas of ornate pattern with stronger colours or metallic paint

5 This design has many uses, and you can vary the colour of the jar and the shape and size of the tree. A row of trees in jars along a hallway will have an imposing effect.

Stencilling on aged or antique wood, with no priming or sanding, can quickly transform anything — even a garden shed.

9

10

11

Cut the holding
bridges of Stencil 9
to release the poppy
flower within the
ginger jar. The poppy
can then be used on
its own, or over the
top of the ginger jar
after it has been
stencilled (see p. 18).

12   Trace the guidelines from this page onto the plastic stencil sheet. Cut along the vertical line of perforations that attaches the
sheet to the book. Cut out and number each stencil. Place each one on card before removing any remaining infills with a scalpel.

Laurel Tree & Ginger Jar Variations

POPPY BORDER: STENCIL 9

Make sure the poppies are equidistant (see "Spacing", p. 5); then mask off the bead border on the ginger jar with two strips of straight-edged paper

LAUREL LEAF & DIAMOND BORDER: STENCILS 8, 11

To keep the leaves at the same angle, draw two horizontal lines and make sure the tips of the leaves and stems are touching them

TERRACOTTA JARS: STENCILS 9, 22

Add each lid after you stencil the main jar, using their common rim for alignment

LINKED LAUREL LEAVES: STENCILS 10, 11

Try to keep the line of stems flowing –
draw a horizontal line as a guide

JASMINE LEAF & BEAD BORDER: STENCIL 9

TOPIARY TREE :
STENCILS 9, 10, 11, 12

JASMINE LEAF & LAUREL BORDER: STENCIL 9, 11

Shorten the
stem for a
different, more
compact look

Experiment
with changing
the shape of the
topiary tree

LAUREL WREATH: STENCIL 10, 11

A central plumb line, lightly pencilled
in here, helps maintain symmetry

This noble laurel wreath is
typical of what is known as
"Napoleonic" design – it
would look striking in a
dining room, stencilled in
gold on a dark background

Traditionally, the
wreath is thicker
at the sides than at
the top and base

Rope & Rose Swag

"SOFT THE SOUL OF LOVE IT BREATHES", wrote the ancient Greek poet Sappho of the rose, and the flower still symbolizes love and perfect beauty. Garlands and wreaths were used in Greek festivities, and during the same historical era (about 600 BC), the Persians perfected the manufacture of rose perfumes. The Romans scattered petals at banquets and made rose water for bathing and for fountains. Another custom in the West was the hanging of a rose over a dining table, which meant that all shared confidences were to be regarded as sacred. As a symbol of love, the rose motif is certainly appropriate for a bedroom, and the swags could be festooned in a dining room to conjure up an image of feasts and elegant banquets.

To create a more delicate, antique look, gently rub over the dry rose stencil with fine wire wool.

Pencil in a horizontal line on the wall, and mark where the repeat bows will go; place the centre of the knot on the line

WIDTH OF SWAG (approx. 75 cm, or 30 in)

To stretch the design, increase the distance between the bows; place Stencil 14B below the centre point

Stencil the rose and rosebud (mask off the stalk)

Mask off the rest of the roses (Stencil 14A)

1 *Do a practice stencil of the rose swag, the bow, and the rope on lining paper first. Use this to measure the area to be stencilled, calculating the number of swags you will need. Mark the centre of each bow-knot along a horizontal line on the wall. Dab in all the bows (Stencil 13) first.*

2 *Using a pencil, mark the centre of the swag at a depth of 30 cm (12 in) below the horizontal line. Mask off Stencil 14A, and position Stencil 14B on the wall at this mark. Dab in the lightest colours of the flowers first, then build up the darker areas; use the same technique for the leaves.*

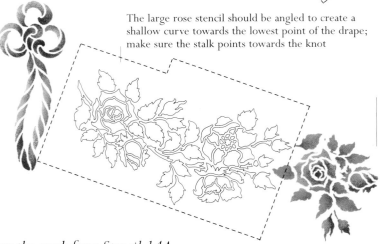

The large rose stencil should be angled to create a shallow curve towards the lowest point of the drape; make sure the stalk points towards the knot

Avoid a wide gap between motifs

If space is tight, you can close up this gap completely, and omit the rope; use as many or as few twists as you need

You could complete the design by adding tassels here

3 *Remove the mask from Stencil 14A. Place the complete rose stencil to the right of the central rose, angling it to create a gentle curve up towards the bow. Stencil, then blot dry, and flip it over.*

4 *Make sure the stencil on the left side of the central rose mirrors the angle of the roses on the right. Avoid wide gaps between motifs: the leaves and buds should interlock.*

5 *Fill in the gap between the bow and the roses with the rope (Stencil 15); you can vary the length by masking or adding one or two sections. Flip the stencil so that the pointed end always faces the roses.*

13

14A

14B

15

Trace the guidelines from this page onto the plastic stencil sheet.
Cut along the vertical line of perforations that attach the sheet
to the book. Cut out and number each stencil. Place each one on
card before removing any remaining infills with a scalpel.

Rope & Rose Swag Variations

ROSE TREE & GINGER JAR:
STENCILS 9, 12, 14A, 14B

ROSE TRELLIS: STENCILS 7, 14A, 14B

Where the diamonds are close
to the roses, stencil more faintly

Draw a circle to
guide you (the
diameter of the
rose tree is about
50 cm, or 20 in);
stencil the central
rose cluster first,
and let the other
roses spiral out

Stencil the base of the trellis first,
stencilling only the bottom half of
the base diamonds

Build up the climbing roses, creating
winding stems, then complete the top
half of the base diamonds

Measure the centre point between
the roses, and mark a point about
5 cm (2 in) below this for the tassel

ROSE & TASSEL SWAG: STENCILS 14A, 15, 30

ROSE & ROPE SWAG: *STENCILS 13, 14A, 14B, 30*

Use the leaves from Stencil 14A

Use 14A below the rope swag, and 14B above

ROSE WREATH:
STENCILS 14A, 14B, 30

Use two sets of buds to finish off the wreath

ROSE & TASSEL SPRAY:
STENCILS 13, 14A, 14B, 30

Use 14B (the rose and rosebud) at the top, then place 14A on each side

Start with the central bow and build the design around it

This design could be stencilled on canvas and used as a base design for needlework or cross-stitch – it would make a lovely cushion or quilt

For a realistic, dramatic effect, create a great range of contrast between leaf highlights and depth of shadow – use a more pointed sponge to speckle deep colours in shadowed areas

Draw a central plumb line to help keep the design symmetrical, and place the tassel on the line

Victorian Leaves & Lilies

THE ELEGANCE OF ACANTHUS FOLIAGE — bold, flowing lines and large, serrated leaves — has long been admired. The name derives from a Greek word *ake* ("sharp point "), which describes the thistle-like leaves the Greeks carved in stone and marble to decorate the tops of columns. During the Renaissance, the revival of classicism reintroduced acanthus foliage; later the Victorians used this motif in fabrics and wallpaper. Another ancient floral motif is the lily, which, in Greco-Roman mythology, was thought to have come from the milk of the goddess Hera/Juno. Long associated with purity and innocence, the lily was used by medieval painters as the emblem of the Virgin Mary. Because they were greatly influenced by medievalism, a group of late Victorian painters — the Pre-Raphaelite Brotherhood — also loved the lily.

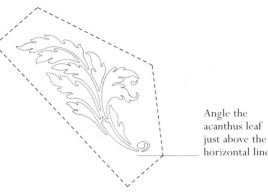

Angle the acanthus leaf just above the horizontal line

1 Draw a horizontal base-line. Using a plumb line, pencil in a central vertical line. Position and stencil the acanthus leaf (Stencil 20) to the left of the vertical line.

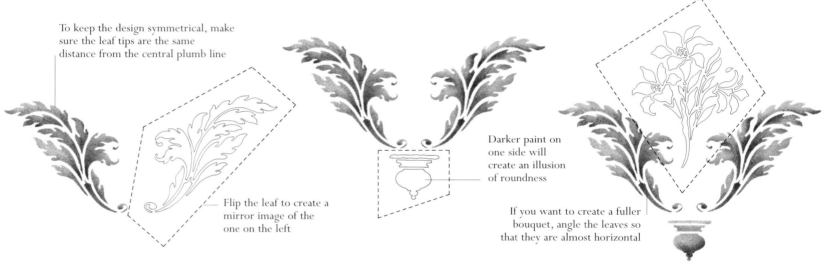

To keep the design symmetrical, make sure the leaf tips are the same distance from the central plumb line

Flip the leaf to create a mirror image of the one on the left

Darker paint on one side will create an illusion of roundness

If you want to create a fuller bouquet, angle the leaves so that they are almost horizontal

2 Blot the stencil well; when it is dry, flip it to create another leaf on the right. Be sure that the angle is the same so that you have a symmetrical design.

3 Place the finial (Stencil 19) under the centre point between the two leaves, and dab in paint; you can create a more rounded finial if you darken one side.

4 Centre the lily (Stencil 18) slightly above the two acanthus leaves. To create a fuller look, stencil more flowerheads between the lower part of the leaves.

5 This spare and elegant design would work well on a centre door panel, or on the headboard of a bed, or to decorate the front and top of a large chest.

The acanthus twist gives elegant definition to beams, pelmets, and door frames; the lily fits a cheese board.

16

17

18

Trace the guidelines from this page onto the plastic stencil sheet. Cut along the vertical line of perforations that attaches the sheet to the book. Cut out and number each stencil. Place each one on card before removing any remaining infills with a scalpel.

19

20

Victorian Leaf & Lily Variations

SINGLE LILY BORDER: STENCIL 18

Measure the distance from one leaf tip to the next, mark these points on a horizontal line, and stencil the upward-facing lilies first; strive for a flowing, graceful line

LEAFY BORDER: STENCIL 17

ACANTHUS TWIST: STENCILS 16, 19, 20

Lengthen or shorten the pole sections as needed

LEAVES, LILIES & TASSELS: STENCILS 18, 20, 30

WINGED ACANTHUS: STENCILS 17, 19, 20

Strengthen the colour of the stems at the centre of the design

For this design, and the one to the right, work from a central plumb line

Several of these sprays stencilled in a row are easy to do, and will create an imposing design; you can omit the motif at top centre for speed and simplicity

LEAF & TASSEL BORDER: STENCILS 13, 20, 30

POLE & LILIES: STENCILS 16, 18, 19

For a more abundant look, stencil the complete trio of lilies above the pole — you can also stencil them hanging down

LEAFY SQUARE: STENCIL 17

This design works well around door handles or along a chest of drawers

POLE & LEAVES: STENCILS 16, 19, 20

The pole is a perfect motif for creating a dado rail

LAUREL & LILY BORDER: STENCILS 10, 18

This would be a pretty design for a bedroom — lightly pencil two horizontal lines and stencil between them to keep the lilies at the same angle

LILY & DIAMOND BORDER: STENCILS 8, 18

WIDE LEAFY BORDER: STENCIL 17

This design is simple to do — even working in only one colour will produce a rich decorative border

Mix & Match

JUST AS THE MOST BEAUTIFUL BOUQUETS are usually made up of an extravagant variety of flowers, you can create your own stunning designs by combining the stencils in this book in any way you wish. The project shown here is based on violets, flowers that are not only favourites of courting couples – they were also adopted by members of a secret society who supported Napoleon's return to power during his exile; members wore violets in order to recognize each other, so the group became known as the *violetta*. Whatever flowers you choose to fill the bowls, you can easily re-create nature's abundance.

The stems should finish 5 cm (2 in) above the line

pencil line

1 Decide where the top edge of the bowl will be, and pencil a horizontal line. Measure 5 cm (2 in) above this line, and stencil the violets (Stencil 31) so that their stems finish at this point.

Flip the stencil for this flower

Angle the stencil slightly, making sure the stems just touch a horizontal base-line

Mask off one flower to fill the small gap; make sure the stems remain above the line

2 Blot the stencil before turning it over, and stencil violets to the left of the first bunch. Blot again, then place the violets at a slight angle to the right of the first bunch, and stencil. Keep the design symmetrical.

3 Mask off Stencil 31 so that only one flower and stalk is visible, and stencil in the gap underneath the central violets; if the gap you have left is smaller than the one shown here, put in the bud.

4 Now stencil in the bowl (Stencil 22) under the violets. The top edge of the bowl should reach just below the horizontal line that you drew in Step 1.

For accurate positioning, draw a horizontal base-line for the border (measure your practice stencil)

5 Continue to stencil several bowls of violets along the whole length of the wall, leaving the same space between each one. To finish, dab in the border (Stencil 24) just under the bowls, leaving a small gap.

6 This is the completed design. If you would like a neat finish to the border, dab in the boxed-leaf motif (Stencil 21) at either end; a slightly different colourway might be effective.

The curved shape of the violet bouquet fits easily in the arch of the cabinet doors.

21

22

23

Trace the guidelines from this page onto
the plastic stencil sheet. Cut along the
vertical line of perforations that
attaches the sheet to the book.
Cut out and number each
stencil. Place each one on
card before removing
any remaining
infills with a
scalpel.

24

25

26

27

28

29

30

31

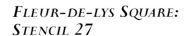

Mix & Match Variations

FLEUR-DE-LYS SQUARE: STENCIL 27

This classic French motif would work well with the irises (Stencil 1) and violets (Stencil 31)

This motif would add a Gothic look to walls or furniture

FLEUR-DE-LYS BORDER: STENCIL 27

LEAFY FLEUR-DE-LYS BORDER: STENCILS 17, 27

IRIS & VIOLET KNOT: STENCILS 1, 13, 27, 31

Align the central iris and the bow along a pencilled plumb line

ART NOUVEAU SQUARE: STENCILS 4, 9, 22, 23

Use Stencil 4 to extend the sides and base of the frame

Decide on the height and width of the frame, and stencil the corners first

Stencil the central knot first, then cut a mask slightly bigger than the bow and place on the iris stencil

The elegant curving motif contrasts well with the boxed leaves

LAUREL & BOXED-LEAF BORDER: STENCILS 10, 21, 27

LAUREL & LILY SWAG: STENCILS 11, 13, 18, 30

You could stencil this design on plain fabric blinds — continue the tassel motif by attaching real tassel pulls

ART NOUVEAU FRAME: STENCILS 1, 4, 13, 23, 30

After you stencil the central motif, do the frame — make sure the corners are placed symmetrically, then fill in the sides and base with Stencil 4

FLEUR-DE-LYS & VIOLETS: STENCILS 27, 31

This pretty motif looks lovely on bedroom furniture, and works well pointing up or down

LATTICE WITH BUTTERFLIES: STENCILS 5, 7, 28, 29, 31

Art Editor **Wendy Bartlet**

Senior Editor **Christine Murdock**

Managing Art Editor **Steve Knowlden**

Managing Editor **Ian Whitelaw**

Production **Meryl Silbert**

DTP Designer **Matthew Greenfield**

The authors would like to thank their families and good friends for all their support — especially Jimmy Yang.

Dorling Kindersley would like to thank photographers Andy Crawford, Steve Gorton, Gary Ombler, and Christine Donnier-Valentin, and stylist Jenny Norton

The Liquitex® acrylic paints used for the projects in this book are distributed in the UK by Colart Fine Art & Graphics, Whitefriars Avenue, Harrow, Middlesex HA3 5RH

First published in Great Britain in 1997
by Dorling Kindersley Limited,
9 Henrietta Street, London WC2E 8PS

2 4 6 8 10 9 7 5 3

A CIP catalogue record for this book is available from the British Library.

ISBN 0-7513-1081-6

Reproduced by Bright Arts, Hong Kong

Printed and bound in Singapore by Imago